THE
BEST
OF
Gourmet

THE
BEST
OF

Gourmet
1988 EDITION

ALL OF THE BEAUTIFULLY
ILLUSTRATED MENUS FROM 1987
PLUS OVER 500 SELECTED RECIPES

FROM THE EDITORS OF GOURMET

CONDÉ NAST BOOKS
RANDOM HOUSE
NEW YORK

LIBRARY OF CONGRESS CATALOGING-IN-PUBLICATION DATA (Revised for vol. 3)

Main entry under title:
The Best of Gourmet.
    Includes indexes.
        1. Cookery, International. I. Gourmet.
TX725.A1B4827   1986   641.5   87-640167
ISBN 0-394-55258-X (v. 1)
ISBN 0-394-56039-6 (v. 2)
ISBN 0-394-56955-5 (v. 3)
Most of the recipes and all the menus in this work were previously published in *Gourmet* Magazine.

Manufactured in the United States of America

98765432   24689753   23456789

First Edition

Grateful acknowledgment is made to the following for permission to reprint recipes previously published in *Gourmet* Magazine.

Nancy Barr: ''Quaresimali'' (page 239). Copyright © 1987 by Nancy Barr. Reprinted by permission of the author.

Marion Cunningham: ''Bridge Creek Fresh Ginger Muffins'' (page 100); ''Cinnamon Butter Puffs'' (page 101); ''Lemon Yogurt Muffins'' (page 100); ''Raw Apple Muffins'' (page 99). Copyright © 1987 by Marion Cunningham. Reprinted by permission of the author.

Barbara Kafka: ''Yellow Cake Layers'' (page 233); ''Chocolate Frosting'' (page 234). Copyright © 1987 by Barbara Kafka. Reprinted by permission of the author.

Faye Levy: ''Chocolate-Flecked Macadamia Nut Torte'' (page 225); ''Macadamia Macaroons'' (page 237); ''Macadamia Mousse Cake'' (page 230); ''Mushroom Macadamia Tart'' (page 185). Copyright © 1987 by Faye Levy. Reprinted by permission of the author.

Sally Tager: ''Burnt Sugar Ice Cream with Chocolate Bits'' (page 246); ''Burnt Sugar Walnut Squares'' (page 234). Copyright © 1987 by Sally Tager. Reprinted by permission of the author.

PROJECT STAFF

For Condé Nast Books

Jill Cohen, Director
Jonathan E. Newhouse, Special Consultant
Ellen Bruzelius, Project Manager
Kristine Smith, Project Assistant
Margarita Smith, Project Assistant
Diane Pesce, Composition Production Manager
Serafino J. Cambareri, Quality Control Manager

For *Gourmet* Magazine

Jane Montant, Editor-in-Chief
Evie Righter, Editor, Gourmet Books
Kathleen Nilon, Project Editor
Romulo Yanes, Staff Photographer
Irwin Glusker, Design Consultant

Produced in association with
Media Projects, Incorporated

Carter Smith, Executive Editor
Judy Knipe, Managing Editor
Charlotte McGuinn Freeman, Assistant Editor
Wm. J. Richardson Associates, Inc., Indexer
Michael Shroyer, Art/Production Director

The editors would like to thank the following people for valuable services rendered for *The Best of Gourmet—1988:* Georgia Chan Downard for her helpful and creative assistance in once again compiling ''A Gourmet Addendum,'' and Blair Brown Hoyt.

The text of this book was set in Times Roman by the Composition Department of Condé Nast Publications, Inc. The four-color separations were done by The Color Company, Seiple Lithographers, and Kordet Graphics. The book was printed and bound by R. R. Donnelley & Sons. Text paper is 80-pound Plainwell Gloss.

Frontispiece: ''Insalata Tonnato'' (page 198).

CONTENTS

INTRODUCTION

s promised, this, the third annual edition of *The Best of Gourmet,* continues *Gourmet* Magazine's tradition of excellence. Although we have not changed the format, we have added a few refinements, including a unique Addendum featuring lighter fare. This volume represents the best of *Gourmet* and more.

The Best of Gourmet is divided into two parts. Part One, The Menu Collection, includes all of the menus from the issues of the past year, arranges them seasonally, and illustrates them with over 75 magnificent color photographs. This year's menus focus on the many wonderful ways to entertain and offer a particularly engaging range of possibilities. If you are feeling ambitious, or, if you have the inclination (and hours) to spend an afternoon in the kitchen, make and enjoy our remarkable *coulibiac,* admittedly time-consuming, but well worth it. If you are feeling slightly less ambitious but no less discerning, whip up our delectable fettuccine with bell peppers, Montrachet, and garlic oil. Or, should you be feeling adventurous, dine, as we did in 1987, *al fresco.* Take just one of our picnics—a tailgate—which features chili bean soup, London broil with ravigote sauce, and chocolate orange marble cake. Another of our picnics, of completely different ambiance, suggests a background of flowering violets as you sample new asparagus and butter-roasted Cornish hens while sipping a rosé of Cabernet Sauvignon. Clearly something special happens when you venture outside.

Something equally exciting happens when you entertain indoors, especially at holiday times. This year not only are the traditional holiday foods represented—tangerine-glazed turkey with sausage, apple, and apricot stuffing for Thanksgiving and crown roast of smoked pork with wild rice, fennel, and sausage stuffing for Christmas—but we have new suggestions, like Louisiana chicken courtbouillon with saffron, destined to become favorites in your holiday cooking repertoire.

Gourmet has always displayed an incomparable ability to read the culinary crystal ball—to know what readers are thinking about even before they fully realize it themselves. A perfect example is our inclusion, this year, of two Afternoon Teas, featuring both sweet and savory treats and reflecting our readers' renewed interest in this Old World tradition.

To render *The Best of Gourmet* the kind of volume you will use over and over, we have, again, included page-number cross references for all of the recipes, referring the reader in The Menu Collection from photograph to recipe or, in A Recipe Compendium, from recipe to photograph.

Part Two, A Recipe Compendium, includes not only all of the Menus and Cuisine Courante recipes presented in Part One, but the best of the recipes from *Gourmet*'s other food feature columns: Gastronomie sans Argent, In Short Order, and Last Touch. This year, recipes from our new column, Microwave Mastery, are represented as well.

In addition to the basic recipes and procedures called for throughout the book, plus new combinations based upon those recipes, our Gourmet Addendum has a new feature this year that we hope you will find exciting. In keeping with the times, we've created many new recipes around a central theme: foods that are intrinsically good for you—pasta, whole grains, and fruits.

The final feature of *The Best of Gourmet* is an appendix of multiple indexes, each fully cross-referenced to make locating any recipe easy: a General Index, a Recipe Title Index, and an Index of 45-Minute Recipes. There is also a listing of Table Setting Acknowledgments, describing all the objects appearing in the photographs.

The Best of Gourmet is a book to treasure. With its meticulous attention to detail and style, it is a source of inspiration season after season, occasion after occasion. In short, *The Best of Gourmet* represents in remarkable fashion the tradition of excellence and good living that is *Gourmet.*

Jane Montant
Editor-in-Chief

PART ONE

THE MENU COLLECTION

The Menu Collection, an extravaganza of brilliant photography, illustrates twelve months of *Gourmet*'s Menus and Cuisine Courante columns. These pages of glorious color have been collected to inspire you, without further ado, to turn to A Recipe Compendium, Part Two, to locate the recipes and re-create these feasts.

The menus themselves range from the informal to elegant, from the basic to challenging, and from the simple to elaborate. The themes are diversified and intended to amuse. Relish Breakfast in Bed—yes, we believe there is still such a luxury—starring parsley shirred eggs and ham biscuits, but celebrate a New Year's Eve Midnight Supper with a glass or two of bubbly and apricot-glazed ham with *orzo* gratin. Or, should something as Old World and wonderful as taking tea be your pleasure, you will find a choice: tea, not for two, but two teas, one for spring, one for fall. Open-faced tea sandwiches and jam tartlets will be among the many tempting offerings.

Gourmet menus also anticipate your entertaining needs, whether you are inviting two or twenty. An early summer Hors d'Oeuvres Buffet, for fifteen or more and perfect for a graduation celebration or special wedding anniversary, features curried chicken on chips, cold roast tenderloin of beef with jellied horseradish cream, and Greek pizza made with *phyllo*. We suggest how it can be prepared in advance to maximize your own good time at the party. You might also start planning, right now, a summer Family Reunion. With our menu and your gathering, the event will be memorable.

Cuisine Courante menus are designed for people "on the run," busy cooks with less time to prepare elaborate meals. One such, a Spring Dinner, stars lamb ragout with spring vegetables that can, for the most part, be prepared up to two days in advance, as can butter-roasted Cornish hens, the main attraction at our Picnic Among the Violets. The intent of this column is to provide simple, contemporary menus and recipes that require a minimum of effort but yield a maximum of flavor.

This volume could hardly be called "the best of" without *Gourmet*'s holiday menus, including an Easter Luncheon, two Thanksgiving menus, a Christmas caroling party, and a festive Christmas dinner. Our formal Thanksgiving dinner starts with saffron shrimp and scallops with biscuit garlands, is followed by tangerine-glazed turkey with sausage, apple, and apricot stuffing and giblet gravy, and ends with spectacular pumpkin bourbon raisin ice cream in walnut lace cups. In keeping with *Gourmet* readers' abiding interest in different cultures and the current fascination with all things Southwestern, our easier Thanksgiving menu has a Southwestern theme and hightlights roast Cornish game hens with red chili gravy and pumpkin bread pudding with coffee whipped cream. Finally, ring in the Yuletide season with a caroling party, featuring a Louisiana specialty that simmers chicken in rich tomato- and saffron-flavored stock and is served over rice in soup bowls. If that isn't ending on a high enough note, we suggest orange almond trifle for dessert! Or, celebrate Christmas dinner over crown roast of smoked pork with wild rice, fennel, and sausage stuffing and apple mustard sauce and orange *phyllo* napoleons with cranberry syrup.

Each menu is annotated with cross references to the recipes in Part Two, A Recipe Compendium. Each menu also includes beverage suggestions from *Gourmet*'s wine editor, Gerald Asher. His always appropriate and often unexpected suggestions, such as a glass of Old Oloroso Sherry for a late afternoon tea, or a Crémant de Bourgogne, a sparkling wine from Burgundy, as an alternative to Champagne on New Year's Eve, will make all your beverage decisions easy.

Whatever the occasion, be it a veranda luncheon, an elegant dinner party, or a holiday meal shared by family and friends, these menus will provide you with extraordinary options from which to choose. Let all seventy-two pages of magnificent color photography inspire you, cajole you, and remind you of the myriad pleasures of dining. Finally, let this edition of *The Best of Gourmet*, like the two volumes before it, become a treasured resource that you will refer to again and again for years to come.

Lemon Lime Mousse, Cinnamon Crisp Pecans

A MIDNIGHT SUPPER

Paprika Shrimp Butter, p. 86

Cocktails   *Salmon and Green Peppercorn Butter, p. 86*

Crackers   Fennel Crudités

Apricot-Glazed Ham, p. 142

Staton Hills Vineyard   *Maple Mustard Sauce, p. 142*
Yakima Valley
Johannisberg Riesling '85   *Orzo Parsley Gratin, p. 168*

Coleslaw with Hot Caraway Vinaigrette, p. 208

Corn and Molasses Rolls, p. 96

Moët & Chandon White Star   *Lemon Lime Mousse, p. 244*
Extra Dry Champagne

Cinnamon Crisp Pecans, p. 259

Paprika Shrimp Butter, Salmon and Green Peppercorn
Butter, Fennel Crudités, Crackers

Apricot Glazed Ham, Orzo Parsley Gratin, Coleslaw with Hot Caraway Vinaigrette, Corn and Molasses Rolls

Raspberry Oatmeal Lace Cookies, Chocolate Mint Truffles

CUISINE COURANTE

NEW YEAR'S EVE DINNER FOR TWO

Brie and Mushroom Tartlets, p. 154

Crémant de Bourgogne   *Beef, Chicken, and Vegetable Fondue, p. 128*

Curry and Chutney Sauce, p. 129 Roasted Red Pepper Sauce, p. 129

Wild Rice with Carrots and Onions, p. 177

Spinach, Fennel, and Pink Grapefruit Salad, p. 206

Raspberry Oatmeal Lace Cookies, p. 239

Chocolate Mint Truffles, p. 257

Beef, Chicken, and Vegetable Fondue, Curry and Chutney Sauce,
Roasted Red Pepper Sauce, Wild Rice with Carrots and Onions,
Spinach, Fennel, and Pink Grapefruit Salad

Celery Root, Potato, and Gruyère Pancake

A FEBRUARY DINNER
FOR FOUR

Monticello Cellars
Chardonnay '84

Spaghetti Squash with
Tomato Cauliflower Sauce, p. 191

Ridge Vineyards
York Creek
Merlot/Cabernet
Sauvignon '78

Roast Leg of Lamb with Roasted Onions
and Mustard Dill Sauce, p. 145

Celery Root, Potato, and Gruyère Pancake, p. 183

Braided Olive Bread, p. 96

Glazed Lemon Almond Pound Cake, p. 229

Gingered Pineapple and Apricot Compote, p. 254

Spaghetti Squash with Tomato Cauliflower Sauce

Roast Leg of Lamb with Roasted Onions

Glazed Lemon Almond Pound Cake, Gingered Pineapple and Apricot Compote

Garlic Parmesan Toasts, Cioppino

CUISINE COURANTE

HEARTY SOUP AND SALAD SUPPERS

Yellow Split-Pea Soup with Kielbasa, p. 112
Marjoram Croutons, p. 103

Sausal Alexander Valley
Zinfandel '82

Watercress, Romaine, and Radish Salad
with Mustard Vinaigrette, p. 207

Poached Pears with Caramel Sauce, p. 253

Cioppino, p. 126
Garlic Parmesan Toasts, p. 102

Clos du Val Napa Valley
Semillon '83

Celery and Potato Salad with Lemon Mayonnaise, p. 208

Chocolate Pecan Pie Squares, p. 236

Yellow Split-Pea Soup with Kielbasa, Marjoram Croutons,
Watercress, Romaine, and Radish Salad with Mustard Vinaigrette

Chocolate Roll with Cappuccino Cream

A PRETHEATER DINNER

Manhattans

Baked Goat Cheese Walnut Toasts, *p. 93*
Sardine Toasts with Mustard and Dill, *p. 93*

West Park Vineyards
New York State
Chardonnay '85

Braised Chicken and Olives, *p. 147*

Saffron Rice with Pine Nuts and Currants, *p. 177*
Romaine and Endive Chiffonade Salad, *p. 206*

Chocolate Roll with Cappuccino Cream, *p. 226*

Braised Chicken and Olives, Saffron Rice with Pine Nuts and Currants

Manhattans, Baked Goat Cheese Walnut Toasts, Sardine Toasts with Mustard and Dill

Saga Blue Walnut and Deviled Ham Pita Spirals, Carrot and Marmalade Gingerbread
with Gingered Orange Cream Cheese

CUISINE COURANTE

AFTERNOON TEA

Hot Brewed Tea such as
Darjeeling or
Earl Grey

Radish and Sprout Triangles
with Lemon Pepper Mayonnaise, p. 94

Saga Blue Walnut and Deviled Ham Pita Spirals, p. 91

Oatmeal Shortbread Tartlets
with Lemon Curd and Kiwi, p. 241

Carrot and Marmalade Gingerbread
with Gingered Orange Cream Cheese, p. 98

Chocolate Almond Raisin Dipping Biscuits, p. 235

Pecan Sour Cream Coffeecake, p. 233

Radish and Sprout Triangles with Lemon Pepper Mayonnaise, Oatmeal Shortbread
Tartlets with Lemon Curd and Kiwi, Chocolate Almond Raisin
Dipping Biscuits, Pecan Sour Cream Coffeecake

Sweet-and-Sour Beet and Caraway Soup

AN EASTER LUNCHEON

Horseradish Steak Tartare, p. 92

Sweet-and-Sour Beet and Caraway Soup, p. 105

Trakia Bulgarian
Chardonnay '85

Coulibiac with Sour Cream Dill Sauce, p. 116

Romaine and Boston Lettuce Salad
with Mustard Shallot Vinaigrette, p. 206

Lemon Ice Cream in an Almond Meringue Basket, p. 248

Coulibiac with Sour Cream Dill Sauce

Lemon Ice Cream in an Almond Meringue Basket

Strawberry Cookie Tarts

CUISINE COURANTE

A SPRING DINNER

Lamb Ragout with Spring Vegetables, p. 146

Noodles with Toasted Cuminseed, p. 167

Château Grand-Puy-Lacoste
Pauillac '79

Dandelion Salad with Pine Nuts, p. 205

Strawberry Cookie Tarts, p. 243

Lamb Ragout with Spring Vegetables, Noodles with Toasted Cuminseed

A LATE SPRING DINNER

Whiskey Sours

Tapenade-Stuffed Cherry Tomatoes, *p. 94*

Parsnip Crisps, p. 89

Pasta with Vegetables and Soppressata, p. 169

Dolcetto d' Alba '85   *Braised Veal Roast with Parsley, p. 135*

*Roasted Peppers with Parmesan Curls
and Balsamic Dressing, p. 186*

Salt Crescents, p. 97

*Rhubarb Raspberry Charlotte
with Rhubarb Raspberry Sauce, p. 254*

Whiskey Sours, Tapenade-Stuffed Cherry Tomatoes, Parsnip Crisps

Pasta with Vegetables and Soppressata

Braised Veal Roast with Parsley, Roasted Peppers with Parmesan Curls
and Balsamic Dressing, Salt Crescents

Fruit and Cheese

A PICNIC AMONG THE VIOLETS

Firestone Vineyard
Santa Ynez Valley
Rosé of Cabernet Sauvignon

Asparagus with Curried Yogurt Dipping Sauce, p. 179

Butter-Roasted Cornish Hens, p. 151

Bulgur Pilaf with Pine Nuts, Raisins, and Orange Rind, p. 173

Fruit and Cheese

Asparagus with Curried Yogurt Dipping Sauce; Butter-Roasted
Cornish Hens; Bulgur Pilaf with Pine Nuts, Raisins, and Orange Rind

Cornmeal Crêpe Gâteau with Corn and Peppers

GAZEBO DINNERS

Cornmeal Crêpe Gâteaux with Corn and Peppers, p. 173

Pork Tenderloin Amandine, p. 140

Vina Ardanza
Rioja Alta '78

Summer Squash Sauté, p. 192

Cantaloupe Sorbet and Vanilla Ice-Cream Bombe, p. 247

Won Ton Ravioli with Eggplant and Sesame Seeds, p. 171

Vouvray '83

*Paupiettes of Sole with Ham, Shiitake Mushrooms, and
Ginger Shallot Beurre Blanc, p. 120*

Napa Cabbage, Snow Pea, and Carrot Sauté, p. 180

Apricot Mousse Cake, p. 224

CHRISTMAS DINNER

Peppery Lobster Soup with Star Croutons, p. 108

Crown Roast of Smoked Pork
with Wild Rice, Fennel, and Sausage Stuffing, p. 137

Apple Mustard Sauce, p. 215

Clos Pégase Alexander Valley Chardonnay '85

Butternut Squash with Ginger Butter, p. 190

Brussels Sprouts with Lemon Butter, p. 179

Rose Salads, p. 205

Orange Phyllo Napoleons with Cranberry Syrup, p. 242

Papagni Vineyards, California Spumante d'Angelo

Peppery Lobster Soup with Star Croutons

Crown Roast of Smoked Pork with Wild Rice, Fennel, and Sausage Stuffing; Apple Mustard Sauce;
Butternut Squash with Ginger Butter; Brussels Sprouts with Lemon Butter

Orange Phyllo Napoleons with Cranberry Syrup

Orange Almond Trifle

CUISINE COURANTE

A CAROLING PARTY

Prosciutto and Fontina Gougères, p. 90

Château Rahoul
Graves Blanc '85

Louisiana Chicken Courtbouillon with Saffron, p. 149

Parsleyed Rice, p. 176

Green Salad with Cucumbers and Lemon Vinaigrette, p. 205

Orange Almond Trifle, p. 232

Louisiana Chicken Courtbouillon with Saffron, Green Salad with
Cucumbers and Lemon Vinaigrette, Parsleyed Ric

PART TWO

A RECIPE COMPENDIUM

Part Two of *The Best of Gourmet*, A Recipe Compendium, is a collection of over 500 recipes carefully selected from the pages of the 1987 issues of *Gourmet* Magazine. Not only are all of the recipes from the Menus and Cuisine Courante columns included, but recipes from the other food feature columns are represented as well: Gastronomie sans Argent, In Short Order, Last Touch, plus selected recipes from *Gourmet*'s new column, Microwave Mastery.

There are recipes, especially those taken from Gastronomie sans Argent, that are based on fruits and vegetables in season, when they are at their peak of ripeness, their most flavorful, and their lowest price. This year's edition of *The Best of Gourmet* features a wealth of recipes for summer's most plentiful vegetables: zucchini, corn, bell peppers, summer squash, and tomatoes. Superb combinations of these include zucchini boats with corn, tomatoes, and coriander *pesto,* and Middle Eastern lamb-stuffed zucchini with mint yogurt sauce. There are recipes for quick and simple grilled vegetables with basil mayonnaise, a marvelous way to take advantage of summer's bargains and perk up your backyard barbecue at the same time. Quality is not sacrificed but enhanced when less expensive cuts of meat are braised, marinated, or grilled in delicious dishes such as braised spicy orange steak roll, pork, corn, and tomato kebabs with hot red pepper marinade, and sweet Italian sausage with grilled bell pepper sauce. Light entrée and pasta salads, such as layered Mexican salad with coriander *jalapeño* dressing and pasta and vegeta-

ble salad with basil dressing, are both economical and flavorful.

From *Gourmet*'s In Short Order column, we have selected a number of recipes for two that can be prepared in less than forty-five minutes. Drawn from cuisines around the world, these quick combinations, such as lemon chicken *scaloppine* with basil butter sauce and fried scallops with citrus ginger sauce, can be made from readily available ingredients. There are simple, quick, desserts like mocha walnut brownie puddings or peanut mousse with chocolate sauce, perfect options for the busy cook who wants to end a meal with a spectacular but not time-consuming dessert.

Gourmet's new column, Microwave Mastery, addresses the fact that the microwave is here to stay, its having become an invaluable tool for today's busy cooks. Our recipes utilize the microwave to its fullest potential and most satisfactory results. The microwave is particularly useful for making sweets, and this year's edition of *The Best of Gourmet* offers numerous candy and confection recipes, many of which can be prepared in the microwave—just one more reason to look forward to the Christmas season.

This year a number of recipes have been chosen to round out our exceptionally varied selection. For instance, there are recipes for both sweet and savory custards, like *crème brûlée* and sun-dried tomato and Fontina quiche; recipes for delicious breakfast treats like raspberry jam-filled French toast; and a variety of granolas and muesli, among them pistachio and apricot granola and an apple, currant, and pecan muesli. Take the edge off a hot summer's afternoon with our recipes for frozen alcoholic drinks such as mango daquiris, strawberry banana margaritas, and refreshing lemon crystal forty-threes. And not forgotten are foods for holiday giving that will not only make this special season even more special but may begin your own holiday gift-giving traditions.

We have made the exceptional variety of recipes in Part Two readily available by dividing the book into fourteen chapters, subdividing those chapters into categories, and arranging the recipes alphabetically within each category. If you want to locate a recipe quickly, there are three indexes to help you: the General Index, the Index of Recipe Titles, and the Index of 45-Minutes Recipes.

Throughout A Recipe Compendium combinations range from the very casual and simple to the most elegant. But simple and elegant can go together as seen in our special fall Elegant but Easy menu featuring sautéed veal chops with basil orange butter. Most of our recipes can be made from ingredients available at the local supermarket, others may require a shopping excursion to an Oriental market or specialty foods store. There are also authentic re-creations of ethnic dishes like the German classic, *sauerbraten*, and the traditional Irish favorite colcannon. There are old favorites such as apricot-glazed ham, or yellow cake layers with chocolate frosting. And there are ingenious new interpretations that are destined to become new favorites, like pasta pizza, or cornmeal pizzette with Gorgonzola, escarole, and bell peppers.

The concluding chapter of A Recipe Compendium is A Gourmet Addendum. As in previous editions, the 1988 Addendum contains certain basic procedures called for throughout the book plus an exciting new section, created particularly for *The Best of Gourmet*. In keeping with the trend toward healthful lighter eating, this year's Addendum focuses on this theme of nutritious cooking, featuring three especially healthful and appealing food groups—pasta, grains, and desserts using fresh, unaged cheeses and fresh fruits. From these basic ingredients, we have built a variety of recipes. After mastering our easy food processor pasta dough, you can branch out and experiment with our spinach, chili corn, and semolina pasta variations. There are various recipes for dishes containing grains, including an exotic curried vegetable stir-fry, as well as irresistible desserts like blueberry cobbler with cornmeal biscuit topping and *coeur à la crème* with red currant sauce.

These recipes are exciting to read, be they from the menus, recipes for seasonal dishes, recipes for two or twenty, or recipes designed for the microwave. Even more pleasure, however, is to be had planning and cooking this wonderful food. So turn this page and embark on any one of the 500 superb *Gourmet* recipes that follow.

HORS D'OEUVRES, CANAPÉS, AND SPREADS

Cold Roast Tenderloin of Beef
with Jellied Horseradish Cream

a trimmed 3½-pound beef tenderloin, tied and
   halved crosswise, at room temperature
about ⅓ cup coarsely ground black pepper
3 tablespoons vegetable oil
2 envelopes unflavored gelatin
4½ cups sour cream
6 tablespoons bottled horseradish
6 tablespoons minced fresh parsley leaves
watercress sprigs for garnish

Pat dry the tenderloin, coat it on all sides with the
pepper, and sprinkle it with salt. In a roasting pan just
large enough to hold the tenderloin heat the oil over high
heat until it is hot but not smoking and in it brown the
tenderloin on all sides. Roast the tenderloin in the pan in
a preheated 500° F. oven for 15 to 17 minutes, or until a
meat thermometer registers 130° F. for medium-rare
meat, and let it cool to room temperature. *The tenderloin may be roasted 2 days in advance, kept wrapped
well and chilled, and brought to room temperature.*
Line 3 empty 12-ounce frozen orange juice cans with
small plastic bags. In a small saucepan sprinkle the gelatin over ¼ cup cold water and let it soften for 10 minutes. In a bowl stir together the sour cream, the
horseradish, the parsley, and salt to taste, add 1 cup of
the sour cream mixture to the gelatin mixture, and heat
the mixture over moderately low heat, stirring, until the
gelatin is melted. Add the mixture to the sour cream
mixture and stir the mixture well. Spoon the horseradish
cream into the lined cans and chill it, covered, for 2

hours, or until it is firm. *The horseradish cream may be
made 2 days in advance and kept covered and chilled.*
Pull the plastic bags from the cans to remove the horseradish cream, peel off the bags gently, and slice thin the
horseradish cream.
   Slice the tenderloin crosswise about ⅓ inch thick, arrange it on a platter with alternating slices of the horseradish cream, and garnish the platter with the
watercress sprigs. Serves 15 to 20 as an hors d'oeuvre.

PHOTO ON PAGE 45

Beggar's Purses
(Egg Packets with Sour Cream and Watercress)

about 12 scallion greens, each 7 inches long
2 ounces smoked salmon, chopped fine
enough watercress, tough stems discarded,
   chopped, to measure ⅔ cup
¼ cup minced red onion
⅓ cup sour cream
1 recipe egg sheets (about 12, page 86)

In a saucepan of boiling water blanch the scallion
greens for 5 seconds, drain them in a colander, and re-
fresh them under cold water. Drain the scallion greens
again and pat them dry with paper towels. In a bowl
combine the smoked salmon, the watercress, the onion,
and the sour cream. Put 1 tablespoon of the filling in the
center of each egg sheet, gather the egg sheet around it
to enclose it, and tie a scallion green around each
"purse." Serve the beggar's purses at room temperature. Makes about 12 hors d'oeuvres.

Egg Sheets
(Paper-Thin Omelets)

4 large eggs, beaten lightly
1 teaspoon cornstarch
¼ teaspoon salt
vegetable oil for brushing the skillet

In a bowl whisk together the eggs, the cornstarch, the salt, and 1 tablespoon cold water until the mixture is smooth, brush a non-stick skillet measuring 6 inches across the bottom lightly with the oil, and heat it over moderate heat until the oil is hot but not smoking. Half fill a ¼-cup measure with the egg mixture, remove the skillet from the heat, and add the egg mixture, swirling the skillet to coat it evenly. Return the skillet to the heat and cook the egg sheet for 5 seconds, or until it is set. Loosen the edges of the egg sheet with a rubber spatula, turn the egg sheet over, and cook it for 3 seconds. Slide the egg sheet onto a plate and make egg sheets with the remaining mixture in the same manner, brushing the skillet lightly with oil each time. *The egg sheets may be made 1 day in advance and kept covered and chilled.* The egg sheets may be shredded and used as a garnish for spinach salad or clear soups. Makes about twelve 6-inch egg sheets.

Paprika Shrimp Butter

2 teaspoons sweet paprika (preferably
   Hungarian) plus additional for garnish
⅛ teaspoon cayenne, or to taste
1¼ sticks (10 tablespoons) unsalted butter
⅔ pound (about 20) shrimp, shelled, reserving
   the shells, and deveined if desired
½ teaspoon salt
2 large garlic cloves, cooked in boiling water
   for 10 minutes, peeled, and mashed with
   a fork
2 teaspoons fresh lemon juice, or to taste
crackers as an accompaniment

In a heavy skillet cook the paprika and the cayenne in 4 tablespoons of the butter over moderately low heat, stirring, for 1 minute, add the shrimp and the salt, and cook the mixture, covered, over low heat, stirring occasionally, for 2 to 3 minutes, or until the shrimp are just firm. Transfer the shrimp with a slotted spoon to a bowl, reserving 2 of them, chilled, for the garnish, add to the skillet 2 tablespoons of the remaining butter and the re-

served shrimp shells, and cook the shells over moderately low heat, stirring, for 2 minutes. Transfer the shell mixture to a food processor and grind it. Strain the shell mixture through a fine sieve over the shrimp, pressing hard on the solids to extract as much of the butter as possible, let the shrimp mixture cool to room temperature, and in the food processor grind it coarse. Add the garlic, the lemon juice, the remaining 4 tablespoons butter, cut into pieces and softened, and salt to taste and blend the mixture well, but do not purée it. Transfer the shrimp butter to a serving dish, packing it and smoothing the top, and mark the top decoratively with a rubber spatula if desired. Chill the shrimp butter, covered tightly with plastic wrap, for at least 1 hour *and up to 48 hours* and let it stand at room temperature for 30 minutes before serving. Just before serving, dust the tail sections of the 2 reserved shrimp with the additional paprika, arrange the shrimp decoratively on the shrimp butter, and serve the shrimp butter with the crackers. Makes about 1⅓ cups.

PHOTO ON PAGE 11

Salmon and Green Peppercorn Butter

½ pound salmon fillet with the skin or a
   ½-pound salmon steak
1 teaspoon fennel seeds, crushed coarse
1 anchovy fillet
1 tablespoon tomato paste
1 tablespoon drained bottled green
   peppercorns (available at specialty foods
   shops and some supermarkets) plus
   additional for garnish if desired
½ teaspoon freshly grated lemon rind
2 tablespoons Pernod
½ teaspoon salt
1¼ sticks (10 tablespoons) unsalted butter
2 teaspoons fresh lemon juice, or to taste
a decoratively cut lemon slice and a fennel top
   for garnish if desired
fennel *crudités* and crackers as
   accompaniments

Put the salmon in a buttered small heavy casserole just large enough to hold it and top it with the fennel seeds, the anchovy, the tomato paste, 2 teaspoons of the peppercorns, the rind, the Pernod, and the salt. Cover the salmon with 4 tablespoons of the butter, sliced thin, and bake it, covered, in the middle of a preheated 350° F.

oven for 12 to 15 minutes, or until it just barely flakes when tested with a fork. Let the salmon cool in the casserole, covered, for 20 minutes and remove and discard the skin and the bones, if necessary. In a food processor blend coarse the salmon mixture with the pan juices, add the remaining 6 tablespoons butter, cut into pieces and softened, 1 teaspoon of the remaining peppercorns, the lemon juice, and salt to taste, and blend the mixture well, but do not purée it. Transfer the salmon butter to a serving dish, packing it and smoothing the top, and mark the top decoratively with a fork if desired. Chill the salmon butter, covered tightly with plastic wrap, for at least 1 hour *and up to 48 hours* and let it stand at room temperature for 30 minutes before serving. Just before serving garnish the dish with the lemon slice, the fennel top, and the additional peppercorns if desired and serve it with the fennel *crudités* and the crackers. Makes about 1½ cups.

PHOTO ON PAGE 11

Curried Chicken on Chips

2 cups chicken stock (page 112) or canned
   chicken broth
1 whole skinless boneless chicken breast
   (about ¾ pound), halved
½ teaspoon ground cardamom
½ teaspoon ground coriander
½ teaspoon ground cumin
¼ teaspoon ground ginger
¼ teaspoon turmeric
a pinch of cayenne
a pinch of sugar
1 tablespoon vegetable oil
¼ cup mayonnaise
¼ cup plain yogurt
50 ridged potato chips
about 30 red grapes, sliced thin crosswise and
   seeded if necessary, plus additional whole
   grapes for garnish
fresh small coriander leaves

In a small saucepan bring the stock to a boil, add the chicken, and poach it at a bare simmer for 7 minutes. Remove the pan from the heat and let the chicken cool in the stock, covered, for 20 minutes. Transfer the chicken with a slotted spatula to a cutting board, reserving the stock for another use, let it cool to room temperature, and cut it into ½-inch pieces. In a small skillet cook the cardamom, the ground coriander, the cumin, the ginger, the turmeric, the cayenne, and the sugar in the oil over moderately low heat, stirring, for 3 to 5 minutes, or until the mixture is fragrant, and let the mixture cool to room temperature. In a bowl stir together the mayonnaise, the yogurt, and the spice mixture, add the chicken and salt and pepper to taste, and toss the mixture well. *The curried chicken may be made 1 day in advance and kept covered and chilled.* Put a chicken piece on top of each potato chip, arrange 3 grape slices and a coriander leaf decoratively next to it, and transfer the hors d'oeuvres to a tray garnished with the additional grapes and a coriander leaf. Makes 50 hors d'oeuvres.

PHOTO ON PAGE 44

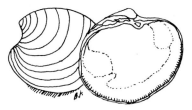

Clams Casino

3 slices of lean bacon
2 tablespoons unsalted butter, cut into
   4 pieces
2 tablespoons minced green bell pepper
2 tablespoons minced scallion
½ teaspoon fresh lemon juice
12 small hard-shelled clams, shucked
   (procedure on page 88), on the half shell

Arrange the bacon in one layer on a double thickness of microwave-safe paper towels on a microwave-safe plate, cover it with a double thickness of microwave-safe paper towels, and microwave it at high power (100%) for 1½ to 2 minutes, or until it is almost cooked but still pliable. In a small microwave-safe bowl microwave the butter at moderately low power (30%) for 15 to 20 seconds, or until it is softened, remove it from the microwave, and blend in the bell pepper, the scallion, and the lemon juice. Arrange the clams hinged side out around the edge of a 9- to 10-inch glass pie plate and divide the butter mixture evenly among them. Quarter the bacon slices crosswise, top each clam with a piece of bacon, and microwave the clams at moderately low power (30%), turning the dish 180° after 3 minutes, for 5 to 7 minutes, or until the clams are just cooked. Makes 12 hors d'oeuvres.

To Shuck Hard-Shelled Clams

Working over a bowl to reserve the liquor hold each clam in the palm of the hand with the hinge against the heel of the palm. Force a strong, thin, sharp knife between the shells, cut around the inside edges to sever the connecting muscles, and twist the knife slightly to open the shells.

If the clams are not to be served raw they may be opened in the oven: Arrange the clams in one layer in a baking pan and put the pan in a preheated 450° F. oven for 3 to 5 minutes, or until the shells have opened. Reserve the liquor and discard any unopened clams.

Salmon Roe Dip with Crudités

6 slices of homemade-type white bread,
    crusts removed
2 tablespoons minced onion
¼ cup fresh lemon juice, or to taste
1 garlic clove, minced
½ pound salmon roe, preferably fresh
    (available at specialty foods shops and
    fish markets)
1 cup olive oil
3 tablespoons snipped fresh dill plus a dill
    sprig for garnish
crudités such as carrot and cucumber slices

Let the bread soak in ⅓ cup water for 5 minutes and squeeze out the excess water. In a blender combine the bread, the onion, the lemon juice, the garlic, and half the salmon roe and blend the mixture until it is smooth. With the machine running add the oil in a slow steady stream and blend the mixture until it is emulsified. *The dip may be made up to this point 2 days in advance and kept covered and chilled.* Transfer the dip to a bowl and stir in the snipped dill and the remaining salmon roe, reserving a teaspoon of roe for garnish. Garnish the dip with the reserved roe and the dill sprig and serve it with the *crudités*. Makes about 3 cups.

PHOTO ON PAGE 45

Greek Pizza

For the phyllo shells
1 stick (½ cup) plus 2 tablespoons unsalted
    butter, melted and kept warm
sixteen 17- by 12-inch sheets of *phyllo*,
    stacked between 2 sheets of wax paper and
    covered with a dampened kitchen towel
For the filling
2 teaspoons minced garlic
3 tablespoons olive oil
¾ pound shrimp (about 20), shelled,
    deveined, and halved lengthwise
1½ tablespoons fresh lemon juice
½ pound Feta, chopped coarse
12 ounces cream cheese at room temperature
1 tablespoon fresh orégano or marjoram
    leaves, minced, or 2 teaspoons dried,
    crumbled
1 green bell pepper, cut into julienne strips
½ cup Kalamata or other brine-cured olives,
    pitted and sliced
6 cherry tomatoes, sliced thin crosswise

Make the *phyllo* shells: Brush lightly with some of the butter 2 baking pans at least 17 inches long, lay 1 sheet of the *phyllo* lengthwise on one of the pans, and brush it lightly with some of the remaining butter. Layer and butter 7 more sheets of *phyllo* over the first sheet in the same manner and roll in the edges on all 4 sides, trimming excess dough at the corners, to form a ½-inch-wide rim. The *phyllo* rectangle should measure about 15 by 7 inches. Brush the rim lightly with some of the remaining butter and prick the bottom of the shell all over with the tip of a knife. Make a second shell on the second baking pan with the 8 remaining *phyllo* sheets and some of the remaining butter in the same manner, reserving 2 tablespoons of the butter in a small saucepan for the filling, and bake the shells in a preheated 400° F. oven, switching their positions in the oven and pressing the centers down gently after 5 minutes, for 10 minutes, or until they are golden. *The shells may be made 1 day in advance and kept covered loosely in a cool dry place.*

Make the filling and assemble the pizzas: Add 1 teaspoon of the garlic to the pan of reserved butter and keep the butter warm. In a skillet heat the oil over high heat until it is hot but not smoking and in it sauté the shrimp, stirring, for 1 minute, or until they begin to turn pink. Add the remaining 1 teaspoon garlic and sauté the mixture, stirring, for 15 seconds. Add the lemon juice and salt and pepper to taste and transfer the mixture to a bowl. *The shrimp may be cooked 1 day in advance, kept covered and chilled, and brought to room temperature.* In a food processor blend the Feta and the cream cheese until the mixture is smooth, sprinkle 1 of the *phyllo* shells with half the orégano, and spoon half the cheese